Key Facts™ on

Canada

~Essential Information on Canada~

By Patrick W. Nee

The Internationalist®

www.internationalist.com

The Internationalist®

International Business, Investment, and Travel

Published by:

The Internationalist Publishing Company

96 Walter Street/ Suite 200

Boston, MA 02131, USA

Tel: 617-354-7722

www.internationalist.com

PN@internationalist.com

Copyright © 2013 by PWN

Table Of Contents

Chapter 1: Background

A land of vast distances and rich natural resources, Canada became a self-governing dominion in 1867 while retaining ties to the British crown. Economically and technologically, the nation has developed in parallel with the US, its neighbor to the south across the world's longest unfortified border. Canada faces the political challenges of meeting public demands for quality improvements in health care, education, social services, and economic competitiveness, as well as responding to the particular concerns of predominantly francophone Quebec. Canada also aims to develop its diverse energy resources while maintaining its commitment to the environment.

Chapter 2: Geography

Location:

Northern North America, bordering the North Atlantic Ocean on the east, North Pacific Ocean on the west, and the Arctic Ocean on the north, north of the conterminous US

Geographic coordinates:

60 00 N, 95 00 W

Map references:

North America

Area:

total: 9,984,670 sq km

country comparison to the world: 2

land: 9,093,507 sq km

water: 891,163 sq km

Area - comparative:

slightly larger than the US

Land boundaries:

total: 8,893 km

border countries: US 8,893 km (includes 2,477 km with Alaska)

note: Canada is the World's largest country that borders only one country

Coastline:

202,080 km

Maritime claims:

territorial sea: 12 nm

contiguous zone: 24 nm

exclusive economic zone: 200 nm

continental shelf: 200 nm or to the edge of the
continental margin

Climate:

varies from temperate in south to subarctic and arctic
in north

Terrain:

mostly plains with mountains in west and lowlands in
southeast

Elevation extremes:

lowest point: Atlantic Ocean 0 m

highest point: Mount Logan 5,959 m

Natural resources:

iron ore, nickel, zinc, copper, gold, lead, rare earth
elements, molybdenum, potash, diamonds, silver,
fish, timber, wildlife, coal, petroleum, natural gas,
hydropower

Land use:

arable land: 4.3%

permanent crops: 0.49%

other: 95.2% (2011)

Irrigated land:

8,699 sq km (2004)

Total renewable water resources:

2,902 cu km (2011)

Freshwater withdrawal (domestic/industrial/agricultural):

total: 42.2 cu km/yr (20%/70%/10%)

per capita: 1,589 cu m/yr (2010)

Natural hazards:

continuous permafrost in north is a serious obstacle to development; cyclonic storms form east of the Rocky Mountains, a result of the mixing of air masses from the Arctic, Pacific, and North American interior, and produce most of the country's rain and snow east of the mountains

volcanism: the vast majority of volcanoes in Western Canada's Coast Mountains remain dormant

Environment - current issues:

air pollution and resulting acid rain severely affecting lakes and damaging forests; metal smelting, coal-burning utilities, and vehicle emissions impacting on agricultural and forest productivity; ocean waters becoming contaminated due to agricultural, industrial, mining, and forestry activities

Environment - international agreements:

party to: Air Pollution, Air Pollution-Nitrogen Oxides, Air Pollution-Persistent Organic Pollutants, Air Pollution-Sulfur 85, Air Pollution-Sulfur 94, Antarctic-Environmental Protocol, Antarctic-Marine Living Resources, Antarctic Seals, Antarctic Treaty, Biodiversity, Climate Change, Desertification, Endangered Species, Environmental Modification, Hazardous Wastes, Law of the Sea, Marine Dumping, Ozone Layer Protection, Ship Pollution, Tropical Timber 83, Tropical Timber 94, Wetlands

signed, but not ratified: Air Pollution-Volatile Organic Compounds, Marine Life Conservation

Geography - note:

second-largest country in world (after Russia); strategic location between Russia and US via north polar route; approximately 90% of the population is concentrated within 160 km of the US border; Canada has more fresh water than any other country and almost 9% of Canadian territory is water; Canada has at least 2 million and possibly over 3 million lakes - that is more than all other countries combined

Chapter 3: People and Society

Nationality:

> <u>noun</u>: Canadian(s)
>
> <u>adjective</u>: Canadian

Ethnic groups:

> British Isles origin 28%, French origin 23%, other European 15%, Amerindian 2%, other, mostly Asian, African, Arab 6%, mixed background 26%

Languages:

> English (official) 58.8%, French (official) 21.6%, other 19.6% (2006 Census)

Religions:

> Roman Catholic 42.6%, Protestant 23.3% (United Church 9.5%, Anglican 6.8%, Baptist 2.4%, Lutheran 2%), other Christian 4.4%, Muslim 1.9%, other and unspecified 11.8%, none 16% (2001 census)

Population:

> 34,568,211 (July 2013 est.)
>
> <u>country comparison to the world</u>: 37

Age structure:

> <u>0-14 years</u>: 15.5% (male 2,753,263/female 2,617,600)
>
> <u>15-24 years</u>: 12.9% (male 2,285,268/female 2,160,005)

25-54 years: 41.4% (male 7,253,587/female 7,067,997)

55-64 years: 13.3% (male 2,285,072/female 2,329,760)

65 years and over: 16.8% (male 2,574,216/female 3,241,443) (2013 est.)

Median age:

total: 41.5 years

male: 40.2 years

female: 42.7 years (2013 est.)

Population growth rate:

0.77% (2013 est.)

country comparison to the world: 136

Birth rate:

10.28 births/1,000 population (2013 est.)

country comparison to the world: 187

Death rate:

8.2 deaths/1,000 population (2013 est.)

country comparison to the world: 91

Net migration rate:

5.65 migrant(s)/1,000 population (2013 est.)

country comparison to the world: 21

Urbanization:

urban population: 81% of total population (2010)

rate of urbanization: 1.1% annual rate of change (2010-15 est.)

Major urban areas - population:

Toronto 5.377 million; Montreal 3.75 million; Vancouver 2.197 million; OTTAWA (capital) 1.208 million; Calgary 1.16 million (2011)

Sex ratio:

at birth: 1.06 male(s)/female

0-14 years: 1.05 male(s)/female

15-24 years: 1.06 male(s)/female

25-54 years: 1.03 male(s)/female

55-64 years: 0.98 male(s)/female

65 years and over: 0.79 male(s)/female

total population: 0.99 male(s)/female (2013 est.)

Maternal mortality rate:

12 deaths/100,000 live births (2010)

country comparison to the world: 150

Infant mortality rate:

total: 4.78 deaths/1,000 live births

country comparison to the world: 182

male: 5.11 deaths/1,000 live births

female: 4.43 deaths/1,000 live births (2013 est.)

Life expectancy at birth:

total population: 81.57 years

country comparison to the world: 13

male: 78.98 years

female: 84.31 years (2013 est.)

Total fertility rate:

1.59 children born/woman (2013 est.)

country comparison to the world: 180

Contraceptive prevalence rate:

74%

note: percent of women aged 18-44 (2002)

Health expenditures:

11.3% of GDP (2010)

country comparison to the world: 15

Physicians density:

1.91 physicians/1,000 population (2006)

Hospital bed density:

3.2 beds/1,000 population (2009)

Drinking water source:

improved:

urban: 100% of population

rural: 99% of population

total: 100% of population

unimproved:

urban: 0% of population

rural: 1% of population

total: 0% of population (2010 est.)

Sanitation facility access:

improved:

urban: 100% of population

rural: 99% of population

total: 100% of population

unimproved:

urban: 0% of population

rural: 1% of population

total: 0% of population (2010 est.)

HIV/AIDS - adult prevalence rate:

0.3% (2009 est.)

country comparison to the world: 80

HIV/AIDS - people living with HIV/AIDS:

68,000 (2009 est.)

country comparison to the world: 49

HIV/AIDS - deaths:

fewer than 1,000 (2009 est.)

country comparison to the world: 80

Obesity - adult prevalence rate:

26.2% (2008)

country comparison to the world: 48

Education expenditures:

5% of GDP (2009)

country comparison to the world: 78

Literacy:

definition: age 15 and over can read and write

total population: 99%

male: 99%

female: 99% (2003 est.)

School life expectancy (primary to tertiary education):

total: 17 years

male: 17 years

female: 17 years (2004)

Unemployment, youth ages 15-24:

total: 14.1%

country comparison to the world: 92

male: 15.9%

female: 12.3% (2011)

Mother's mean age at first birth:

27.6 (2007 est.)

Chapter 4: Government and Key Leaders

Country name:

> <u>conventional long form</u>: none
>
> <u>conventional short form</u>: Canada

Government type:

> a parliamentary democracy, a federation, and a constitutional monarchy

Capital:

> <u>name</u>: Ottawa
>
> <u>geographic coordinates</u>: 45 25 N, 75 42 W
>
> <u>time difference</u>: UTC-5 (same time as Washington, DC during Standard Time)
>
> <u>daylight saving time</u>: +1hr, begins second Sunday in March; ends first Sunday in November
>
> <u>note</u>: Canada is divided into six time zones

Administrative divisions:

> 10 provinces and 3 territories*; Alberta, British Columbia, Manitoba, New Brunswick, Newfoundland and Labrador, Northwest Territories*, Nova Scotia, Nunavut*, Ontario, Prince Edward Island, Quebec, Saskatchewan, Yukon*

Independence:

1 July 1867 (union of British North American colonies); 11 December 1931 (recognized by UK per Statute of Westminster)

National holiday:

Canada Day, 1 July (1867)

Constitution:

made up of unwritten and written acts, customs, judicial decisions, and traditions; the written part of the constitution consists of the Constitution Act of 29 March 1867, which created a federation of four provinces, and the Constitution Act of 17 April 1982, which transferred formal control over the constitution from Britain to Canada, and added a Canadian Charter of Rights and Freedoms as well as procedures for constitutional amendments

Legal system:

common law system except in Quebec where civil law based on the French civil code prevails

International law organization participation:

accepts compulsory ICJ jurisdiction with reservations; accepts ICCt jurisdiction

Suffrage:

18 years of age; universal

Executive branch:

head of state: Queen ELIZABETH II (since 6 February 1952); represented by Governor General David JOHNSTON (since 1 October 2010)

head of government: Prime Minister Stephen Joseph HARPER (since 6 February 2006)

cabinet: Federal Ministry chosen by the prime minister usually from among the members of his own party sitting in Parliament

elections: the monarchy is hereditary; governor general appointed by the monarch on the advice of the prime minister for a five-year term; following legislative elections, the leader of the majority party or the leader of the majority coalition in the House of Commons generally designated prime minister by the governor general

Legislative branch:

bicameral Parliament or Parlement consists of the Senate or Senat (105 seats; members appointed by the governor general on the advice of the prime minister and serve until 75 years of age) and the House of Commons or Chambre des Communes (308 seats; members elected by direct, popular vote to serve a maximum of four-year terms) elections: House of Commons - last held on 2 May 2011 (next to be held no later than 19 October 2015)

election results: House of Commons - percent of vote by party - Conservative Party 39.6%, NDP 30.6%, Liberal Party 18.9%, Bloc Quebecois 6%, Greens 3.9%; seats by party - Conservative Party 166, NDP 103, Liberal Party 34, Bloc Quebecois 4, Greens 1

Judicial branch:

highest court(s): Supreme Court of Canada (consists of the chief justice and 8 judges)

note - in 1949, Canada finally abolished all appeals beyond its Supreme Court to the Judicial Committee of the Privy Council (in London)

judge selection and term of office: chief justice and judges appointed by the prime minister in council; all judges appointed for life with mandatory retirement at age 75

subordinate courts: federal level: Federal Court of Appeal; Federal Court; Tax Court; federal administrative tribunals; courts martial; provincial/territorial: provincial superior, appeals, first instance, and specialized courts; in 1999, the Nunavut Court - a circuit court with the power of a

superior court and the territorial courts - was
established to serve isolated settlements

Political parties and leaders:

Bloc Quebecois [Daniel PAILLE]

Conservative Party of Canada [Stephen HARPER]

Green Party [Elizabeth MAY]

Liberal Party [Robert RAE (interim)]

New Democratic Party or NDP [Thomas MULCAIR]

Political pressure groups and leaders:

other: agricultural sector; automobile industry;
business groups; chemical industry; commercial
banks; communications sector; energy industry;
environmentalists; public administration groups; steel
industry; trade unions

International organization participation:

ADB (nonregional member), AfDB (nonregional
member), APEC, Arctic Council, ARF, ASEAN
(dialogue partner), Australia Group, BIS, C, CD,
CDB, CE (observer), EAPC, EBRD, EITI
(implementing country), FAO, FATF, G-20, G-7, G-
8, G-10, IADB, IAEA, IBRD, ICAO, ICC (national
committees), ICRM, IDA, IEA, IFAD, IFC, IFRCS,
IGAD (partners), IHO, ILO, IMF, IMO, IMSO,
Interpol, IOC, IOM, IPU, ISO, ITSO, ITU, ITUC

(NGOs), MIGA, MINUSTAH, MONUSCO, NAFTA, NATO, NEA, NSG, OAS, OECD, OIF, OPCW, OSCE, Paris Club, PCA, PIF (partner), UN, UNAMID, UNCTAD, UNESCO, UNFICYP, UNHCR, UNMISS, UNRWA, UNTSO, UPU, WCO, WFTU (NGOs), WHO, WIPO, WMO, WTO, ZC

Diplomatic representation in the US:

chief of mission: Ambassador Gary DOER

chancery: 501 Pennsylvania Avenue NW, Washington, DC 20001

telephone: [1] (202) 682-1740

FAX: [1] (202) 682-7726

consulate(s) general: Atlanta, Boston, Buffalo, Chicago, Dallas, Denver, Detroit, Los Angeles, Miami, Minneapolis, New York, San Francisco/Silicon Valley, Seattle

consulate(s): Anchorage (AK), Houston, Palo Alto (CA), Philadelphia, Phoenix, Raleigh (NC), Salt Lake City, San Diego, Tucson

Diplomatic representation from the US:

chief of mission: Ambassador David C. JACOBSON

embassy: 490 Sussex Drive, Ottawa, Ontario K1N 1G8

mailing address: P. O. Box 5000, Ogdensburg, NY 13669-0430; P.O. Box 866, Station B, Ottawa, Ontario K1P 5T1

telephone: [1] (613) 688-5335

FAX: [1] (613) 688-3082

consulate(s) general: Calgary, Halifax, Montreal, Quebec City, Toronto, Vancouver, Winnipeg

Key Leaders:

Governor Gen.	David JOHNSTON
Prime Min.	Stephen Joseph HARPER
Min. of Aboriginal Affairs & Northern Development	Bernard VALCOURT
Min. of Agriculture & Agri-Food	Gerry RITZ
Min. of Canadian Heritage & Official Languages	Shelly GLOVER
Min. of the Canadian Northern Economic Development Agency	Leona AGLUKKAQ
Min. of Citizenship &	Chris

Immigration	ALEXANDER
Min. of the Economic Development Agency of Canada for the Regions of Quebec	Denis LEBEL
Min. of Employment & Social Development	Jason KENNEY
Min. of the Environment	Leona AGLUKKAQ
Min. for the Federal Economic Development Initiative for Northern Ontario	Greg RICKFORD
Min. of Finance	James Michael FLAHERTY
Min. of Fisheries & Oceans	Gail SHEA
Min. of Foreign Affairs	John Russell BAIRD
Min. of Health	Rona AMBROSE
Min. of Industry	James MOORE
Min. of Infrastructure, Communities, &	Denis LEBEL

Intergovernmental Affairs	
Min. of Intl. Development	Christian PARADIS
Min. of Intl. Trade	Edward FAST
Min. of Justice & Attorney Gen.	Peter MACKAY
Min. of Labor	Kellie LEITCH
Min. of National Defense	Robert NICHOLSON
Min. of National Revenue	Kerry-Lynne FINDLAY
Min. of Natural Resources	Joe OLIVER
Min. of Public Safety & Emergency Preparedness	Steven BLANEY
Min. of Public Works & Govt. Services	Diane FINLEY
Min. for Status of Women	Kellie LEITCH
Min. of Transport	Lisa RAITT

Min. of Veterans Affairs	Julian FANTINO
Min. of State (Agriculture)	Maxime BERNIER
Min. of State (Atlantic Canada Opportunities Agency)	Rob MOORE
Min. of State (Democratic Reform)	Pierre POILIEVRE
Min. of State (Federal Economic Development Agency for Southern Ontario)	Gary GOODYEAR
Min. of State (Finance)	Kevin SORENSON
Min. of State (La Francophonie)	Christian PARADIS
Min. of State (Multiculturalism)	Tim UPPAL
Min. of State (Science & Technology)	Greg RICKFORD
Min. of State (Seniors)	Alice WONG
Min. of State (Small Business & Tourism)	Maxime BERNIER

Min. of State (Social Development)	Candice BERGEN
Min. of State (Sport)	Bal GOSAL
Min. of State (Western Economic Diversification)	Michelle REMPEL
Min. of State of Foreign Affairs & Consular	Lynne YELICH
Min. of State & Chief Govt. Whip	John DUNCAN
Pres., Treasury Board	Anthony Peter CLEMENT
Leader of the Govt. in the House of Commons	Peter VAN LOAN
Leader of the Govt. in the Senate	Marjory LEBRETON
Governor, Bank of Canada	Stephen POLOZ
Ambassador to the US	Gary DOER
Permanent Representative to the UN, New York	Guillermo RISHCHYNSKI

Flag description:

two vertical bands of red (hoist and fly side, half width) with white square between them; an 11-pointed red maple leaf is centered in the white square; the maple leaf has long been a Canadian symbol; the official colors of Canada are red and white

National symbol(s):

maple leaf

National anthem:

name: "O Canada"

lyrics/music: Adolphe-Basile ROUTHIER [French], Robert Stanley WEIR [English]/Calixa LAVALLEE

note: adopted 1980; originally written in 1880, "O Canada" served as an unofficial anthem many years before its official adoption; the anthem has French and English versions whose lyrics differ; as a Commonwealth realm, in addition to the national anthem, "God Save the Queen" serves as the royal anthem (see United Kingdom)

Chapter 5: Economy

Economy - overview:

As an affluent, high-tech industrial society in the trillion-dollar class, Canada resembles the US in its market-oriented economic system, pattern of production, and affluent living standards. Since World War II, the impressive growth of the manufacturing, mining, and service sectors has transformed the nation from a largely rural economy into one primarily industrial and urban. The 1989 US-Canada Free Trade Agreement (FTA) and the 1994 North American Free Trade Agreement (NAFTA) (which includes Mexico) touched off a dramatic increase in trade and economic integration with the US its principal trading partner. Canada enjoys a substantial trade surplus with the US, which absorbs about three-fourths of Canadian exports each year. Canada is the US's largest foreign supplier of energy, including oil, gas, uranium, and electric power. Given its great natural resources, highly skilled labor force, and modern capital plant, Canada enjoyed solid economic growth from 1993 through 2007. Buffeted by the global economic crisis, the economy dropped into a sharp recession in the final months of 2008, and Ottawa posted its first fiscal deficit in 2009 after 12 years of surplus. Canada's major banks, however, emerged from the financial crisis of 2008-09 among the strongest in the world, owing to the financial sector"s tradition of conservative lending practices and strong capitalization. Canada achieved marginal growth in 2010-12 and plans to balance the budget by 2015. In addition, the country"s petroleum sector is rapidly becoming an even larger economic driver with Alberta"s oil sands significantly boosting Canada"s proven oil reserves, ranking the country third in the world behind Saudi Arabia and Venezuela.

GDP (purchasing power parity):

$1.513 trillion (2012 est.)

country comparison to the world: 14

$1.485 trillion (2011 est.)

$1.448 trillion (2010 est.)

note: data are in 2012 US dollars

GDP (official exchange rate):

$1.819 trillion (2012 est.)

GDP - real growth rate:

1.8% (2012 est.)

country comparison to the world: 142

2.6% (2011 est.)

3.2% (2010 est.)

GDP - per capita (PPP):

$43,400 (2012 est.)

country comparison to the world: 19

$43,100 (2011 est.)

$42,500 (2010 est.)

note: data are in 2012 US dollars

GDP - composition by sector:

agriculture: 1.7%

industry: 28.5%

services: 69.8% (2012 est.)

Labor force:

18.89 million (2012 est.)

country comparison to the world: 32

Labor force - by occupation:

agriculture: 2%

manufacturing: 13%

construction: 6%

services: 76%

other: 3% (2006 est.)

Unemployment rate:

7.3% (2012 est.)

country comparison to the world: 81

7.5% (2011 est.)

Population below poverty line:

9.4%

note: this figure is the Low Income Cut-Off (LICO), a calculation that results in higher figures than found in many comparable economies; Canada does not have an official poverty line (2008)

Household income or consumption by percentage share:

lowest 10%: 2.6%

highest 10%: 24.8% (2000)

Distribution of family income - Gini index:

32.1 (2005)

country comparison to the world: 103

31.5 (1994)

Investment (gross fixed):

24% of GDP (2012 est.)

country comparison to the world: 56

Budget:

revenues: $682.5 billion

expenditures: $749.5 billion (2012 est.)

Taxes and other revenues:

37.5% of GDP (2012 est.)

country comparison to the world: 54

Budget surplus (+) or deficit (-):

-3.7% of GDP (2012 est.)

country comparison to the world: 133

Public debt:

84.6% of GDP (2012 est.)

country comparison to the world: 23

83.4% of GDP (2011 est.)

note: figures are for gross general government debt, as opposed to net federal debt; gross general government debt includes both intragovernmental debt and the debt of public entities at the sub-national level

Inflation rate (consumer prices):

1.5% (2012 est.)

country comparison to the world: 30

2.9% (2011 est.)

Central bank discount rate:

1% (31 December 2010 est.)

country comparison to the world: 141

0.25% (31 December 2009 est.)

Commercial bank prime lending rate:

3% (31 December 2012 est.)

country comparison to the world: 176

3% (31 December 2011 est.)

Stock of narrow money:

$654.1 billion (31 December 2012 est.)

country comparison to the world: 9

$585 billion (31 December 2011 est.)

Stock of broad money:

$1.523 trillion (31 December 2012 est.)

country comparison to the world: 13

$1.404 trillion (31 December 2011 est.)

Stock of domestic credit:

$3.083 trillion (31 December 2012 est.)

country comparison to the world: 9

$2.836 trillion (31 December 2011 est.)

Market value of publicly traded shares:

$1.907 trillion (31 December 2011)

country comparison to the world: 7

$2.16 trillion (31 December 2010)

$1.681 trillion (31 December 2009)

Agriculture - products:

wheat, barley, oilseed, tobacco, fruits, vegetables; dairy products; fish; forest products

Industries:

transportation equipment, chemicals, processed and unprocessed minerals, food products, wood and paper products, fish products, petroleum and natural gas

Industrial production growth rate:

1.8% (2012 est.)

country comparison to the world: 102

Current account balance:

-$59.92 billion (2012 est.)

country comparison to the world: 190

-$48.91 billion (2011 est.)

Exports:

$462.9 billion (2012 est.)

country comparison to the world: 13

$461.4 billion (2011 est.)

Exports - commodities:

motor vehicles and parts, industrial machinery, aircraft, telecommunications equipment; chemicals, plastics, fertilizers; wood pulp, timber, crude petroleum, natural gas, electricity, aluminum

Exports - partners:

US 74.5%, China 4.3%, UK 4.1% (2012)

Imports:

$474.8 billion (2012 est.)

country comparison to the world: 11

$460.4 billion (2011 est.)

Imports - commodities:

machinery and equipment, motor vehicles and parts, crude oil, chemicals, electricity, durable consumer goods

Imports - partners:

US 50.6%, China 11%, Mexico 5.5% (2012)

Reserves of foreign exchange and gold:

$68.55 billion (31 December 2012 est.)

country comparison to the world: 31

$65.82 billion (31 December 2011 est.)

Debt - external:

$1.326 trillion (31 December 2012)

country comparison to the world: 15

$1.191 trillion (31 December 2011)

Stock of direct foreign investment - at home:

$918.7 billion (31 December 2012 est.)

country comparison to the world: 8

$873.3 billion (31 December 2011 est.)

Stock of direct foreign investment - abroad:

$953.3 billion (31 December 2012 est.)

country comparison to the world: 9

$899.3 billion (31 December 2011 est.)

Exchange rates:

Canadian dollars (CAD) per US dollar

0.9992 (2012 est.)

0.9895 (2011 est.)

1.0302 (2010 est.)

1.1431 (2009)

1.0364 (2008)

Fiscal year:

1 April - 31 March

Chapter 6: Energy

Electricity - production:

580.6 billion kWh (2010 est.)

country comparison to the world: 8

Electricity - consumption:

504.8 billion kWh (2009 est.)

country comparison to the world: 9

Electricity - exports:

43.91 billion kWh (2010 est.)

country comparison to the world: 5

Electricity - imports:

18.79 billion kWh (2010 est.)

country comparison to the world: 9

Electricity - installed generating capacity:

131.5 million kW (2009 est.)

country comparison to the world: 8

Electricity - from fossil fuels:

28.8% of total installed capacity (2009 est.)

country comparison to the world: 181

Electricity - from nuclear fuels:

10.1% of total installed capacity (2009 est.)

country comparison to the world: 20

Electricity - from hydroelectric plants:

57% of total installed capacity (2009 est.)

country comparison to the world: 35

Electricity - from other renewable sources:

3.9% of total installed capacity (2009 est.)

country comparison to the world: 44

Crude oil - production:

3.592 million bbl/day (2011 est.)

country comparison to the world: 7

Crude oil - exports:

1.355 million bbl/day (2009 est.)

country comparison to the world: 12

Crude oil - imports:

791,100 bbl/day (2009 est.)

country comparison to the world: 16

Crude oil - proved reserves:

173.6 billion bbl (1 January 2012 est.)

country comparison to the world: 4

Refined petroleum products - production:

1.978 million bbl/day (2009 est.)

country comparison to the world: 11

Refined petroleum products - consumption:

2.259 million bbl/day (2011 est.)

country comparison to the world: 12

Refined petroleum products - exports:

437,300 bbl/day (2009 est.)

country comparison to the world: 19

Refined petroleum products - imports:

282,200 bbl/day (2009 est.)

country comparison to the world: 25

Natural gas - production:

160.1 billion cu m (2011 est.)

country comparison to the world: 5

Natural gas - consumption:

103.3 billion cu m (2011 est.)

country comparison to the world: 8

Natural gas - exports:

92.72 billion cu m (2011 est.)

country comparison to the world: 6

Natural gas - imports:

30.49 billion cu m (2011 est.)

country comparison to the world: 15

Natural gas - proved reserves:

1.727 trillion cu m (1 January 2012 est.)

country comparison to the world: 22

Carbon dioxide emissions from consumption of energy:

548.8 million Mt (2010 est.)

country comparison to the world: 10

Chapter 7: Communications

Telephones - main lines in use:

18.201 million (2011)

country comparison to the world: 16

Telephones - mobile cellular:

27.387 million (2011)

country comparison to the world: 37

Telephone system:

general assessment: excellent service provided by modern technology

domestic: domestic satellite system with about 300 earth stations

international: country code - 1; submarine cables provide links to the US and Europe; satellite earth stations - 7 (5 Intelsat - 4 Atlantic Ocean and 1 Pacific Ocean, and 2 Intersputnik - Atlantic Ocean region) (2011)

Broadcast media:

2 public TV broadcasting networks each with a large number of network affiliates; several private-commercial networks also with multiple network affiliates; overall, about 150 TV stations; multi-channel satellite and cable systems provide access to

a wide range of stations including US stations; mix of public and commercial radio broadcasters with the Canadian Broadcasting Corporation (CBC), the public radio broadcaster, operating 4 radio networks, Radio Canada International, and radio services to indigenous populations in the north; roughly 2,000 licensed radio stations in Canada (2008)

Internet country code:

.ca

Internet hosts:

8.743 million (2012)

country comparison to the world: 14

Internet users:

26.96 million (2009)

country comparison to the world: 16

Chapter 8: Transportation

Airports:

>1,453 (2012)

>country comparison to the world: 4

Airports - with paved runways:

>total: 522

>over 3,047 m: 19

>2,438 to 3,047 m: 20

>1,524 to 2,437 m: 148

>914 to 1,523 m: 257

>under 914 m: 78 (2012)

Airports - with unpaved runways:

>total: 931

>1,524 to 2,437 m: 72

>914 to 1,523 m: 387

>under 914 m: 472 (2012)

Heliports:

>27 (2012)

Pipelines:

>gas 835 km; liquid petroleum 75,000 km (2010)

Railways:

>total: 46,552 km

>country comparison to the world: 5

standard gauge: 46,552 km 1.435-m gauge (2008)

Roadways:

total: 1,042,300 km

country comparison to the world: 6

paved: 415,600 km (includes 17,000 km of expressways)

unpaved: 626,700 km (2008)

Waterways:

636 km (Saint Lawrence Seaway of 3,769 km, including the Saint Lawrence River of 3,058 km, shared with United States) (2011)

country comparison to the world: 78

Merchant marine:

total: 181

country comparison to the world: 35

by type: bulk carrier 62, cargo 15, carrier 1, chemical tanker 15, combination ore/oil 1, container 2, passenger 5, passenger/cargo 63, petroleum tanker 11, roll on/roll off 6

foreign-owned: 19 (Estonia 1, France 1, Netherlands 1, Norway 4, Sweden 2, US 10)

registered in other countries: 225 (Australia 5, Bahamas 96, Barbados 11, Cambodia 2, Cyprus 2, Honduras 1, Hong Kong 77, Liberia 2, Malta 5,

Marshall Islands 8, Norway 1, Panama 6, Spain 4, Vanuatu 5) (2010)

Ports and terminals:

Fraser River Port, Halifax, Hamilton, Montreal, Port-Cartier, Quebec City, Saint John (New Brunswick), Sept-Isles, Vancouver

oil terminals: Lower Lakes terminal

Chapter 9: Military

Military branches:

> Canadian Forces: Canadian Army, Royal Canadian
> Navy, Royal Canadian Air Force, Canada Command
> (homeland security) (2011)

Military service age and obligation:

> 17 years of age for voluntary male and female
> military service (with parental consent); 16 years of
> age for Reserve and Military College applicants;
> Canadian citizenship or permanent residence status
> required; maximum 34 years of age; service
> obligation 3-9 years (2012)

Manpower available for military service:

> males age 16-49: 8,031,266
> females age 16-49: 7,755,550 (2010 est.)

Manpower fit for military service:

> males age 16-49: 6,633,472
> females age 16-49: 6,389,669 (2010 est.)

Manpower reaching militarily significant age annually:

> male: 218,069
> female: 206,195 (2010 est.)

Military expenditures:

> 1.1% of GDP (2005 est.)

Chapter 10: Transnational Issues

Disputes - international:

managed maritime boundary disputes with the US at Dixon Entrance, Beaufort Sea, Strait of Juan de Fuca, and the Gulf of Maine including the disputed Machias Seal Island and North Rock; Canada and the United States dispute how to divide the Beaufort Sea and the status of the Northwest Passage but continue to work cooperatively to survey the Arctic continental shelf; US works closely with Canada to intensify security measures for monitoring and controlling legal and illegal movement of people, transport, and commodities across the international border; sovereignty dispute with Denmark over Hans Island in the Kennedy Channel between Ellesmere Island and Greenland; commencing the collection of technical evidence for submission to the Commission on the Limits of the Continental Shelf in support of claims for continental shelf beyond 200 nautical miles from its declared baselines in the Arctic, as stipulated in Article 76, paragraph 8, of the United Nations Convention on the Law of the Sea

Illicit drugs:

illicit producer of cannabis for the domestic drug market and export to US; use of hydroponics technology permits growers to plant large quantities of high-quality marijuana indoors; increasing ecstasy production, some of which is destined for the US; vulnerable to narcotics money laundering because of its mature financial services sector

Map of Canada

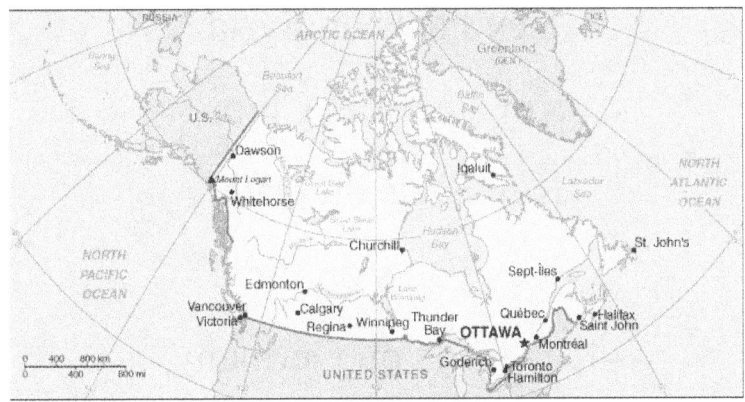

Other Key Facts™ Titles

Key Facts on Malaysia

Key Facts on Vietnam

Key Facts on Hong Kong

Key Facts on Jordan

Key Facts on Australia

Key Facts on Venezuela

THE INTERNATIONALIST®

2013

WWW.INTERNATIONALIST.COM

www.ingramcontent.com/pod-product-compliance
Lightning Source LLC
Chambersburg PA
CBHW071644170526
45166CB00003B/1431